Living Things and Their Habitats

Welcome to the Pond

by Ruth Owen

Ruby Tuesday Books

Published in 2016 by Ruby Tuesday Books Ltd.

Editor: Mark J. Sachner
Designer: Emma Randall
Consultant: Judy Wearing, PhD, BEd
Production: John Lingham

Photo credits
Alamy: 11 (bottom), 19 (top right), 26 (left); Corbis: 29; FLPA: 8 (left), 9, 14, 15 (left), 16, 27; Nature Picture Library: 22–23; Public Domain: 13 (top right); Science Photo Library: 20–21; Shutterstock: Cover, 2–3, 4–5, 6–7, 8 (right), 10, 11 (top), 12, 13, 15, 16, 18–19, 24–25, 26 (right), 28, 30–31.

British Library Cataloguing in Publication Data (CIP)
is available for this title.

ISBN 978-1-910549-73-5

Printed in India

www.rubytuesdaybooks.com

Contents

Words shown in **bold** in the text are explained in the glossary.

Welcome to the Pond

Who and what lives in a pond?

This **habitat** is home to many different types of plants.

The residents of this habitat include dragonflies, frogs, ducks and other animals.

Every living thing in the pond gets what it needs to live from its habitat.

A pond is a type of ecosystem. An ecosystem includes all the living things in an area. It also includes non-living things such as water, soil, rocks and sunlight. Everything in an ecosystem has its own part to play.

So let's find out what happens in this habitat...

...welcome to the pond!

Pond Plants

It's spring, and the plants that live in the pond are growing new **shoots** and leaves.

Water lilies grow in the muddy soil at the bottom of the pond.

They take in water and **nutrients** from the mud through their roots.

Each water lily stem grows up to the surface of the pond.

At the end of the stem is a leaf, or lily pad, that floats on the surface.

Lily pad

Stems underwater

A moorhen hunts for insects, snails and seeds on floating lily pads.

Water cabbage plants don't grow in soil. They float on the pond with their roots dangling below the surface. The roots take in water and nutrients from the pond water.

A water cabbage floating on a pond

Roots

Water cabbage

In what ways are pond plants useful to the animals that live in this habitat?

Pond Plants for Dinner

At the edge of the pond, tall bulrush plants grow in the mud.

Water vole

Flower spike

A little water vole feeds on the bulrushes, grass, and other plants that grow around the pond.

A bulrush plant can grow to be 3 m tall. Its leaves look like giant blades of grass. It grows fat, soft, brown flower spikes.

Water vole

Burrow entrance

Pond weed

Water voles dig homes, called burrows, in the banks of streams, rivers and ponds.

How do you think the bulrushes are helpful to a mother duck?

Meet a Duck Family

Safe among the bulrush stems is a duck's nest.

The mother duck hid her eggs from foxes, rats and other animals that eat eggs.

Duck eggs

A duck makes her nest from leaves and grass. She also uses soft feathers that she plucks from her body. She lays up to 12 eggs in the nest.

Now the ducklings are hatching from their eggs.

In less than a day, the baby ducks are ready to go swimming.

They follow their mother into the water and start feeding on plants and insects.

This duckling has just hatched.

Mother duck

There's something green floating on the pond. What could it be?

Mini Pond Plants

The pond is home to thousands of tiny plants called duckweed.

The plants float on the water.

Fish, ducks and other water birds eat duckweed.

Duckweed sticks to the feet and feathers of ducks. When the birds walk or fly from one pond to another, the tiny plants go, too. This helps duckweed spread to new places.

Some duckweed plants have a leaf-like body.

Other types are shaped like tiny, green footballs.

Each tiny green ball is a single plant!

Leaf-like duckweed plants

What else lives on the surface of the pond?

Insect Life at the Pond

Many different types of insects live on or near a pond.

Pond skaters are insects that look as if they are skating across the water's surface.

They hunt for insects that fall into the water and cannot escape.

Whirligig beetle

A pond skater eating a drowned wasp

Whirligig beetles spin and whirl in circles on the water's surface. These beetles also feed on insects that fall into the pond. Like pond skaters, they help clean up the pond by eating dead insects.

Dragonflies are large, flying insects that lay their eggs in ponds and lakes.

A dragonfly lowers the tip of her body into the water.

Then she lays hundreds of eggs in the pond.

A female dragonfly laying eggs

A close-up photo of dragonfly eggs

What other animal do you think lays its eggs in the pond?

It's Time for Tadpoles

A female frog has laid about 2000 eggs in the pond.

Frog

The tiny black eggs are inside jelly.

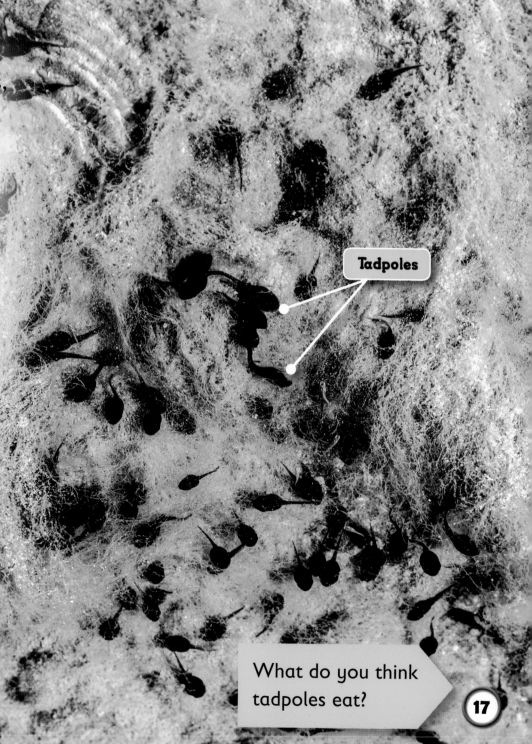

After two weeks, baby frogs, called tadpoles, hatch from the eggs.

Adult frogs breathe air, but tadpoles only breathe underwater.

This is why a frog lays her eggs in a pond or lake.

Tadpoles

Like fish, tadpoles take in **oxygen** from the water through body parts called **gills**.

What do you think tadpoles eat?

What's That Floating on the Pond?

The pond is home to green, plant-like living things called **algae**.

Some types of algae grow in long strands that are thinner than a human hair.

Tadpoles feed on algae and water plants. Fish, snails, ducks and other pond animals also eat algae.

Tadpoles eating algae growing on a rock.

Hair-like algae

These close-up photos were taken with a microscope.

Some algae are so tiny, that a single one can only be seen using a **microscope**.

When lots of algae floats on a pond, the water looks like slimy, green soup!

This alga is about 200 times bigger than in real life.

Tadpoles also feed on zooplankton. What do you think this is?

Microscopic Pond Creatures

A pond is home to billions of tiny animals called zooplankton.

Some zooplankton can just about be seen with your eyes.

They look like tiny specks moving in the water.

Other zooplankton are so small, they can only be seen with a microscope.

Zooplankton are food for tadpoles, fish, insects and other pond residents.

Microscopic zooplankton and green algae in pond water

Zooplankton feed on algae and each other. Some zooplankton work as a pond clean-up crew. They eat the poo and dead bodies of other pond animals.

Algae

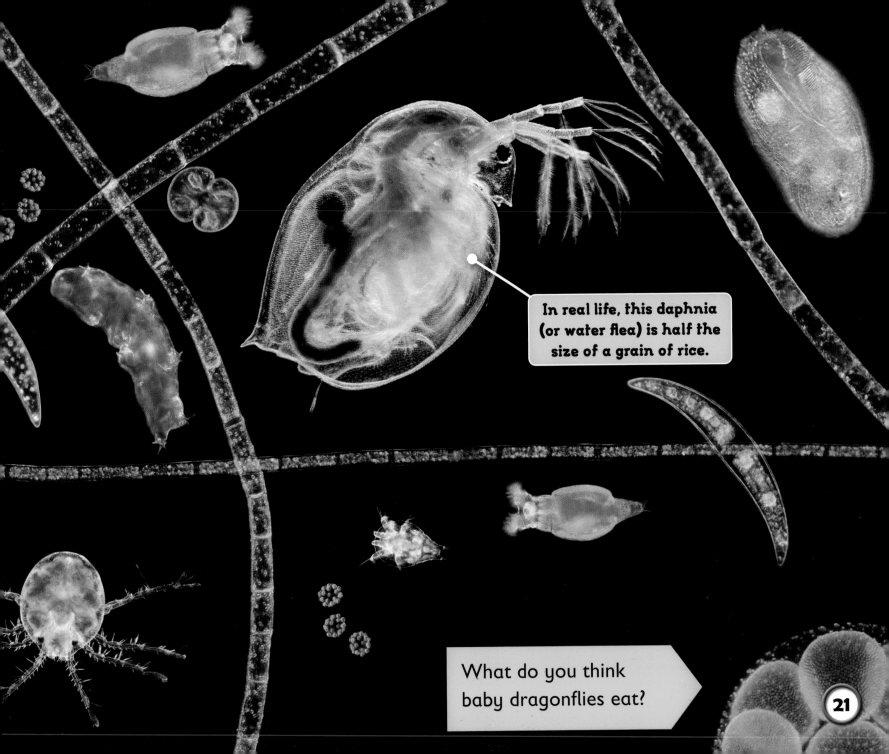

In real life, this daphnia (or water flea) is half the size of a grain of rice.

What do you think baby dragonflies eat?

Little Hunters

It's been three weeks since the dragonfly laid her eggs in the pond.

Now, baby dragonflies, called **nymphs**, are hatching from the eggs.

Tadpole

Nymph

The nymphs are skilful hunters that catch tadpoles, snails, insects and even small fish.

Nymphs catch their **prey** with their high-speed, grabbing mouthparts.

Mouthparts

Dragonfly nymphs live in water. Unlike adult dragonflies that breathe air, nymphs can only breathe underwater. They breathe through gills—just like tadpoles and fish.

What other animals do you think are hunting at the pond?

Hunters at the Pond

Grass snakes visit the pond to hunt for frogs, toads and fish.

Grass snake

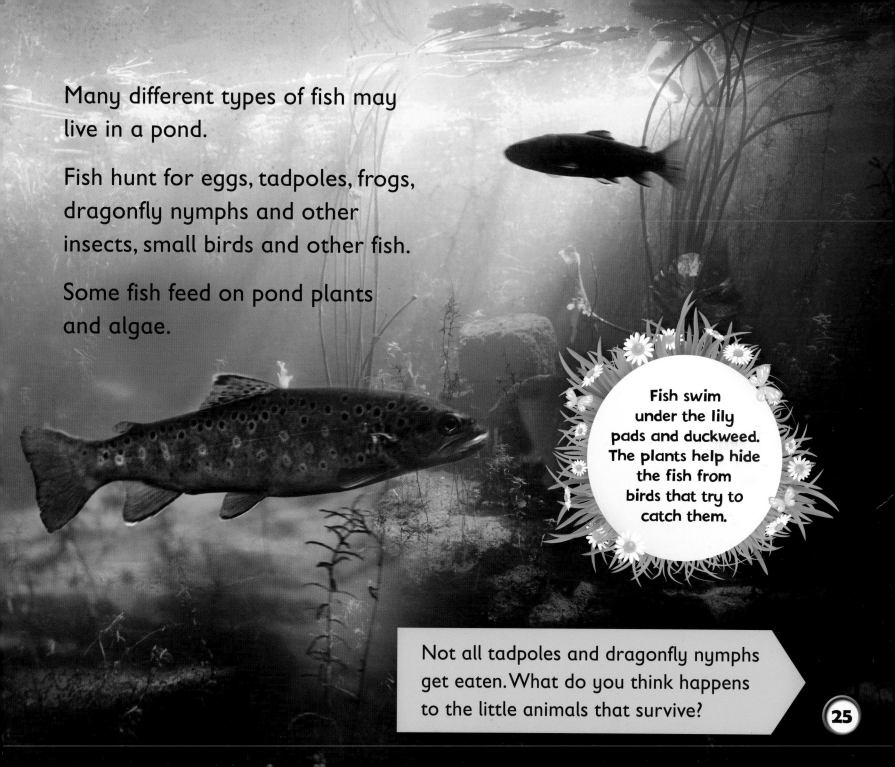

Many different types of fish may live in a pond.

Fish hunt for eggs, tadpoles, frogs, dragonfly nymphs and other insects, small birds and other fish.

Some fish feed on pond plants and algae.

Fish swim under the lily pads and duckweed. The plants help hide the fish from birds that try to catch them.

Not all tadpoles and dragonfly nymphs get eaten. What do you think happens to the little animals that survive?

Big Changes in the Pond

Throughout the summer, the tadpoles have been changing and growing bigger.

Each tadpole has grown four legs and its tail is gone.

Froglet

How a Tadpole Changes

Now the tadpoles have become froglets that can breathe air and live on land.

The dragonfly nymphs have been growing and changing, too.

Finally, a nymph climbs from the water and clings to a plant stem.

Then its new adult dragonfly body breaks free from its old nymph skin.

New dragonfly body

Old nymph skin

Once a nymph becomes a dragonfly, it no longer lives in water. Now it can breathe air through tiny holes in its body. It also has wings and can fly.

What do adult frogs and dragonflies eat?

All Grown Up!

It's late summer, and the pond babies are all grown up.

Dragonflies zoom back and forth over the water, catching flies and other insects.

Dragonfly

The ducklings are now the same size as their mum.

Young ducks

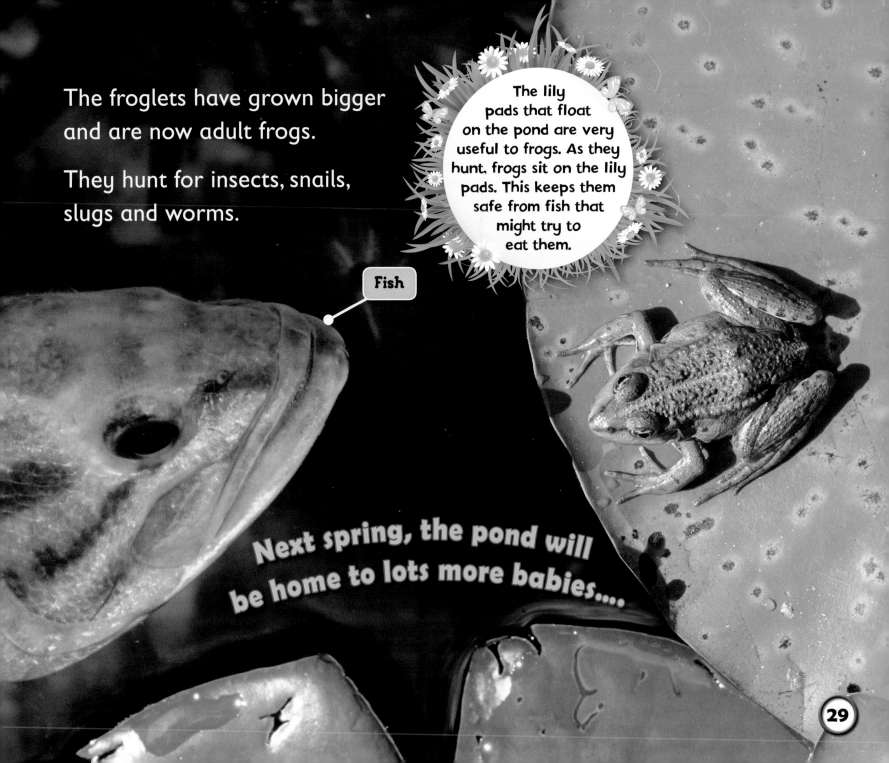

The froglets have grown bigger and are now adult frogs.

They hunt for insects, snails, slugs and worms.

The lily pads that float on the pond are very useful to frogs. As they hunt, frogs sit on the lily pads. This keeps them safe from fish that might try to eat them.

Fish

Next spring, the pond will be home to lots more babies....

A Pond Food Web

A food web shows who eats who in a habitat.

This food web diagram shows the connections between some of the living things in a pond.

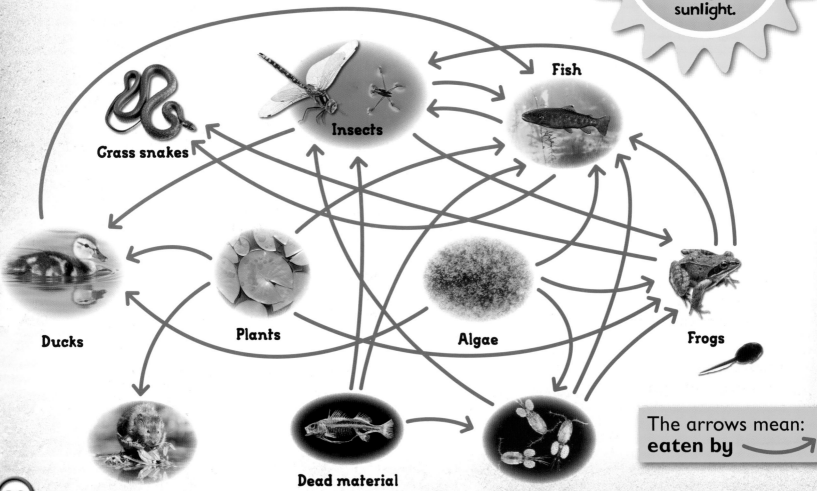

Fish

Insects

Grass snakes

Ducks

Plants

Algae

Frogs

Water voles

Dead material

Zooplankton

The arrows mean: **eaten by**

Glossary

algae
Plant-like living things that mostly grow and live in water. Like plants, algae can make their own food using sunlight. Seaweed is a type of algae.

gills
Body parts that some animals use for breathing underwater. Fish, tadpoles and dragonfly nymphs have gills.

Gills

habitat
The place where living things, such as animals or plants, live and grow. A pond, forest or garden is a type of habitat.

microscope
An instrument used for seeing things that are too small to see with the eyes alone.

nutrient
A substance that a living thing needs to grow, get energy and be healthy.

nymph
A young insect with legs.

oxygen
A gas in air and water that living things need for survival.

prey
An animal that is hunted by other animals for food.

shoot
A new part that grows on a plant. Shoots can become new stems or leaves.

Index

Learn More Online

To learn more about life in a pond, go to
www.rubytuesdaybooks.com/habitats